LIFE and DEATH
in the Valley of the Sagebrush Mariposa Lily

Ehor Boyanowsky

innovativeink
PUBLISHING
A Division of Kendall Hunt

Many thanks to my commissioning editor Angela Lampe and Publishing Specialist Supervisor Lynne Rogers without whose expertise this book would not have been of such high quality.

Cover image © Ehor Boyanowsky
Other photographs in the book by Alexei Boyanowsky, Cristina Martini and the author.

www.innovativeinkpublishing.com
Send all inquiries to:
4050 Westmark Drive
Dubuque, IA 52004-1840

Dedications

For Georgia and Russ
And
For Megan and Charlie

May your lives together be filled with the joy of each other's company

In Memoriam

Erzsabet and Victor Martini

Katarina and Dmitro Boyanowsky

Contents

1

She
Is a match
When struck
Ignites
Flares up
And consumes you

2

To Kyiv with Love

Raptors
The Eastern Imperial eagle, handsome, magnificent in flight
A creature heralded an apex predatory wonder
In reality, a primitive scrounging blunderer
No supernal skills, a plodding hunter
Merely mediocre in spotting and swooping
A clumsy fisher less lightning, more thunder
Whose prime feast is carrion
Sometimes inspired to harass and plunder
The catch of fishers and hunters
Who drop their prey to rush back
To save spouse and nestlings
from the invading hooligan pack
A sinister alliance of convenience
Murderous giants, rats with wings
Shrieking in unseemly, feeble voices, none sings

Their target the osprey smaller, swifter and skilled
A master hunter and fisher
Troubles no other, makes a living
Eating only what he has killed
Fresh from the water into which he has plunged
Deep from his relentless hovering in the skies
Deftly his talons have grasped his still living prize
And to prep for the homebound trip
Rotating it like a rocket in his grip
He flies to the nest and feeds his brood
And spouse and lives a simple life of
Good food, sad views over
Their now ravaged steppe.

He closes his eyes only briefly to rest
How long can they hold out alone?
Now is the time for help from a sister, a brother
Too soon he spots with a shudder
The Janus-faced eagles circling his nest.

3

The Anchoring Child

Two youths buffeted by the upheaval
Of the Aquarian age seek sanctuary in the wild
And find an anchor in their child
Who wanders the woods alone
Through the bush, light and dark.
Calling for them announcing
Without panic she's lost her way
She can't see them though
They are right there
Only feet away
In their sanctuary the wilderness park.

Her father's companion
Each evening in the boat
Dad rows and she trolls
through evenings imbued
With the mournful cry of the loon
Luring above the trees the rising full moon
To illuminate the boreal lake
And celebrate their shared bounty:
The fish they take
Bring home to filet, to savour
To begin the day, reassured
A sign it is them the ancient gods favour.

On the last evening her father
Holds her in his arms
Calling into the compound
From the dismal forest beyond
Two feathered PreCambrian gods hooting
As they waft nearer, unbelievably huge
The sound instills the child with their power

One snowy, ghostlike, the other grizzled, horned
Betraying the fearful thrill rippling through her
She clings tighter to her father as they fly past
So as dad and daughter bid farewell
To the living crucibles of wisdom
She embraces them as her talisman.

4

True Grit

Normally chatty six year old
Became strangely silent when
We approached O'Hare
World's largest
Airport then
To place her on a flight
For a long stay
In Northern Ontario
With aunt and uncle
To their mutual delight.

"Are you okay ?"
We queried
Suddenly worried
She was feeling abandoned by
Self-absorbed Papa and Mumma
Too busy and harried
To detect her trauma.

"I'm fine" she quietly breathed
With her arms folded
She uttered a determined sigh
"Just wondering whether I can read
The right numbers
On that board so high
When I get dropped with my bag
On the street
But I will try."

5

The Pond

A pond in Annapolis Royal town
The ancient settlement of
Henry IV, France's crown
Is many things.
First kidneys of village outflow
And home for muskrat, wood duck, crow
Sculpins, snakes, hawks
Even the occasional ruddy fox.

And in winter the shining
Ice is ideal any day for those who play
Canada's original sport: shinny
With just skates, a stick and puck
No need for an arena wooden or tinny
or a bus, max or minitruck
To drive a dozen padded cherubs
At the break of day to try outs
For peewee or midget make-believe
Pseudo-NHL franchise clubs

So little has changed
Since the Pond provided
For the Order of Good Cheer.
In their second winter of the year 1606
Sport and feast to bring pleasure
To the coldest time of year
In enduring measure.

6

The Pact

He left his mum
Who had slipped in the river
Drying in the sun
To walk downstream
With his dad and his setter
Thompson S Hunter.
For once the family was intact
And he entered the river
Just above the back eddy because
There a steelhead re-starting its journey
To its birthing pool
In Shovelnose Creek
Might pause.

His Dad entered the river
Just below the back eddy
And Thompson stalked
Blue Grouse in the swale
While others
Boomed out mating calls, pounding
On chest drums in lustful travail
Echoing in the Tantalus mountains surrounding.

The world was unfolding as it should
On a spring day punctuated
By avalanches on slopes
From the heat now slick and steep
Until he noticed Thompson
Scurried back to Dad who was waist deep
Casting to the center seam.
Then he saw it: a grizzly streaking
Toward his pup and his dad

Alarmed, he began shrieking
Dad turned first confused suddenly aware
Hurtling towards him a great bear.
And bizarrely went stumbling to shore
Holding his rod in the air
Shouting "Whoa bear!"

Was he trying to save the setter?
Why charge a charging grizzly?
The young man without hesitation
Swam through the deep back eddy
Showing no inkling of self-preservation
And pulled up waders full, spray can at the ready
Behind his dad and placed a hand
On his shoulder.
"I have the bear spray, let's walk around the grizz
Heel Thompson". The bear stood up nose
Caressing the air, confused how it came to this
One romping baby goat and
A strange, grisly creature emerging from the river
Had morphed into three. So he followed, cautiously.

A mile or more as they walked the track grinning
His dad noted: "I always had your back
Now you've had mine." So now a pact by design
Forged instantly, set to last a very long time
The end of an outing. And a beginning.

7

The Fisher Prince

The boy flew over the stones
Under the desert sun.
Ululating in joyous tones
Toward his mum
Triggering alarm
A serpent writhing
In four foot muscular
Shimmering coil
Wrapped around his arm.
A sign an omen
Of the grasp he would gain
Of the world navigating
On his decades long run.

He set out the next day
With only rod
A drink and a bite
And resolve to try
Gone
For three hours
Returning in the crimson twilight
Nonchalantly reporting
Thirteen trout on the fly.

Ten years later 2008
In the ancestral wild
Of the Kamchatkan state
He enables the frail
King of The World Bank to cast
To fish
And is hailed an acolyte
Gaining an invite

Into the kingdom
Of Mammon, alas even
As it is about to ignite,
self-immolate.
So shape shifting
To a muscular coil
He captains yachts
Searching the seas
For his quarry from
Alaska to Caribbean
Until in the end
Finally
He finds solace and succor
And family.
To shift yet again.

8

Midnight Passage

On the Evening of January 12, 1971
Flakes melted on the windshield
As we drove through the silence of snow
Tires crunching and streetlights flickering
In the expectant hours of a night
That drew us into its comforting bosom
Of muffled city sounds
Over the bridge and almost too soon
Into the fluorescent glare of the waiting room

A vigil began as her mum rode
The waxing and waning waves of pain
To a crescendo and an old soul,
spewing fluid to sound her arrival
Wrenched herself from her mother's womb
Eyes flashing and lungs filling the room
Eager to be re-born.

And eager ever since to pursue mystery
Run like the wind and dance like a banshee
Re-inventing her ancient history.

9

Communing Spirit

What was to be her fate?
So many passions so many skills
An ability almost effortlessly
To bring together so many diverse wills
Destined otherwise alas
As strangers
Anonymously merely to pass
Unknown, not to meet
In each other's world or on the street
Nor nurture as sister and brother

Now they do and flourish, sing, drink
And best of all, break bread
With one another.

10

Alchemy

T is for Tory, neurons igniting, energy surging
Enriching planet earth constantly encouraging
All who dwell upon it.
T is for Tom, kind and wise
And thoughtful and laconic.
Marriage the potion
Mixing those elements for
The good of humankind, no doubt.
Including Russell and Benyon
Now united as one, a companion
family spanning north and south.
But handle with caution
The product T'N'T
Is a potent one
Aiming to create in a stable state
Only life-giving emission
No uncontrolled detonation or ignition
Allowed.

11

IOU on Christmas 2022

The Boots
Some couples track their love
In flowers, diamonds or wine
We have those treasures in our trove
Of relationship roots
But the strange aspect of our sublime
Journey together
Is its progression in boots.

First wading boots to join me in braving
The Thompson and others of lesser power
Then Le Chameau the ultimate boot
For Glenmazeran's hills of heather and flower
To hike, to hunker down, to shoot.

And then the exquisite Mexican pair
To stride along in fashionable Vancouver
And attract many an envious stare.

But now for the winter cold
I found you the perfect mode
Korkers. Warm, dry and preventing a fall
And feel cozichka once and for all.

12

PERFECT 10

On a beach after dark
A flashing eyed animal lover
Heard a dictator ordering
A setter to come over
And sit in the park
Whereas he thought he could roam free.
But she joined the tyrant for a glass of wine
And three years later, by design
She, he, Thompson became a family of three.
Now, many years have passed
No catch and release ever after
Joy, tragedy but most of all laughter
Has made this merger last.

13

White Mountain

At six thousand feet
Lush today in winter bleak
Outside my study window
Reminds me
That a drawing by Dmitri
Of a pointy topped peak
Is grounded in reality.
I look at it whenever
I conjure him -
Living on a strand
The continent spanned -
in an ancient land
Captured by him in perpetuity.
*

14

Rudbeckia Triloba

An awkwardly named floral
Found in riparian profusion
Melodically named brown-eyed susan
The glorious perennial
At Nighthawk Ranch
Is the signature flower
We now propose
To name for ferocious
Georgia Cordelia Rose
A dauntless brown-eyed girl
Brilliant and glowing gold
In the garden
A G-force of nature
In the world

15

Uno Duo

She gave me youth
I gave her gin
She offered me passion
I concocted an exotic existence
Laced with laughter, some sin
She promoted initiation
I cultivated procrastination

Which she outfoxed with a ruse
That allowed the sin of sloth
In one realm
So long as I ground my nose
In scribbling production

Her legacy a book writer
Mine a feisty street fighter
Together an alliance
Eliminating ennui
And meeting hostility
Or indifference
With defiance.

16

The Beasts

An urchin eyes burning black tears
fled her mother's wrath
Riding a belching black beast
And overcame her fears
To find again the joy with grandmother
Of those lost infant years.
Eons later
In the desert she plants a tree
In memory of that ancient wisdom
That celebrated her ferocious
Nature
With uncorroded love
That set her free
To ride and defeat
The many beasts that
She faced and slayed
In her stride.

17

Living with the Creatures of Light and Darkness

She loves animals
Brought home snakes and skunks
As a child
Fell for a handsome setter – Thompson S Hunter
On the beach
And snagged an old goat.
Or was he trolling to get her?

Who brought her to a savannah
Where Mr. Martin, the bruin, shared the wild asparagus
And soundless offerings of steaming campana strewn
Throughout the meadow among the sweet clover
Impeccably courteous for years to follow
Until he vanished – retired – to the long rest in his cave
His sarcophagus in Bear Hollow.

Only she describes the slithering rattling viper
Crawling through the campsite
Under verandahs, underfoot and out of sight
As a cute creature rather than terrifying toxic sniper.
And animals love her -
Jake the teenaged turkey histrionic
Followed her into her boudoir
But it turned out to be platonic.
Sad but not heartbroken Jake curled up on the bed
Too soon victim of turkeycide
Loved and long remembered now dead.

And then the bobcat – Robert
Who feeding on Tom one Valentine's Day
She dropped with one shot from her Browning 243

Then cried, then skinned, then ate
The flesh beautiful, the taste first rate.

Each animal an object of awe and curiosity
Spiders – black widow, recluse or wolf
Eight legged or four including Canis lupus:
Siggie howling only once, his baritone
Silencing the coyotes high pitched moan
All treated with affection
Like Edga Raven Poe
Wounded he decided to stay for recuperation
On the woodshed she built for me
The envy of a Thoreau.

18

A Toast

How do we spend our time
Celebrating
The first twelve years of marriage
As we move like the seasons
Toward living together
Everyday
Not just weekends
And not just holidays
But watching the sun rise
And set
And the ospreys
Struggling to make babies and
A life
While bees explore every bit of
Our universe
To feed us, our family
And our world
Its sweet nectar
Ever expanding
In our minds, in our life
In the creatures
Large and small
That everyday
Come to call

19

8/8/09 – 8/8/23 A Celebration Enroute

We had years back gathered at the Wedding Point
Where once decades before
Through their exchange of vows
Thea and Sam had anointed
That patch of savannah on the shore
As a sacred place in family lore.

Fourteen years on we drive for hours
To a rendezvous with fate
So the surgeon can apply his healer's magic
As shaman scientist to dictate, portend
Whether the date will be marked
As a new beginning or an end
To a cycle of life untragic.

20

Then the Whole Becomes Greater Than the Parts

Sometimes Nicola's eyes burn devastatingly
Then she melts into my arms embracing me
Sometimes Josie is lost in thought, cannot hear me
And then her wolf-eyes stare comfortingly
Sometimes Bella is overwhelmed with jealousy
And then rushes outside to protect me
Sometimes Brit won't listen to my pleas
Then finally returns to curl up on my knees

But when we are all here those
Single gestures appear to propose
A life complete in movement and repose.

21

The Needle Nose

Her howling in the cavernous cargo hangar
Chilled your heart
And when you took her out of the cage
She licked your face
And melted that heart
As only giving birth to a child could.

And then nonchalantly
Had a pee of a length
Approaching infinity
And gazed about as only
A budding principessa
Could manage
With enormous dignity

You were her first conquest
Followed quickly by me
And then her consort to be
Thompson S Hunter
Who welcomed this visiting
Royalty but then retreated
Into misery
Upon discovering she
Planned to remain and rule
The domain once his alone
So he retreated from us all
And stared at the wall

Until Nicola sizing up the situation
And having established her station
In the family
Applied her considerable charms
And one day arriving home

We found her locked in his arms
And he at the end
In love so willingly.

So Thompson was not gay
Perhaps sometimes did stray
Or at least swung both ways
But did he have in his advanced age
A reserve of DNA to assuage
The testicular strain of his spontaneous passion?
The birth of a robust Josie Bonaparte
In sixty-some days revealed
That at least one strong swimmer
Did not yield to the ravages of old age
But pierced an egg and produced
A spitting image of her daddy's visage.

So began a reign of intense experience
A full ten years of love and resilience
Against monsters and adversity
And human subjects not properly respectful
Even among many of the faithful
Who immersed themselves
In the brimming joy reservoir
Of the unmatchable chatelaine
Who ruled as Nicola de Beauvoir.

22

From Mountain and Forest

A young girl in the Carpathians
Dreamed of a life filled
With creatures great and small
Wild and savage and giving
that would fill her world with
Feathers and fur and a life
Worth living immersed
In the splendour of the good earth

In the far north of Ontario
A young boy wandered the
Woods and lakes and rivers that
Filled his world with pike and grouse and deer
To fish and hunt and gather and rejoice
In so many lives lived sharing both mirth,
With humankind and even mortal fear
In the splendour of the good earth

And now here in our eleventh year
We share a world and life
That we have etched from the land
And rejoice in our sacred routine
Of pups and birds and animals
Sharing the bounty, giving birth,
In the splendour of the good earth.

23

Catch and Release Not Considered

Strong like bull
Smart like tractor
The ideal woman
My father mused.
But how to attract her?
Troll my setter along the beach
And see her rise to the bait
On our first date
She fell in love - with Thompson
The dog and included me
A welcome fate
For both dog and man
We can't complain
TSH retired to the Okanagan
I toil on with some brain, little brawn
And toast the world as all have heard
With the perfect Martini
Neither shaken nor stirred.

24

And Now For The Future

It is raining and cold
And the memories of all
Junes past
Cast a pall
On a summer
Suddenly on hold

Am I old?
I was just a moment ago
Are you young?
Or merely among
This tribe a spirit
Who ferociously throws
Itself into a life
Neither of us foretold

Preparing to build and soon
To celebrate
Without further urging,
The river, the riparian,
And the savannah now claimed
By the hostages to fortune.

25

Dream Song

You hide in a city guise:
Goretex, cotton, denim and leather
But a flash of midnight fire
Burning embers for eyes
Sounds an alarm
Here lies desire.

First your hands:
Willowy, delicate and brown
Then your arms:
Long, lean and strong
And eager breasts :
Birds released from a pen
Black, tan and silky
Defying gravity
Bursting once again
Into a light that ignites
Desire as they take flight
And set mere mortals on fire.

And I call them in with my voice
And whisper my love
For them, for their keeper
Soon the twilight turns mauve
And my sweet ciorica
Transforms from seeker
To sleeper
The night folds over us
Above and below.
And the moon rolls over us
In her silent elliptical glow.

26

She Conquers

She is spawn of the mountains
And their rivers flowing to the valley
To nurture, to restore
Over steppes that were
The empire of the Mongol heretofore.
It was there she embraced the crows
And Attila and Vlad and
The other ruthless foes
Who swept through her land
And anointed her with the essence of
The Hun and the Jew and the Roman.

Ferocious child distilled from that cauldron of blood
Took flight over land and sea and finally stood
On a new mountain and strand
And anointed this infant kingdom
With ferocious lust to drink its promise
To live and love and kindle trust
In this man
Who rejoices in her passion, her grand plan
And the land and the man
Embrace her with the love
That only she can render
So violent and yet
So tender.

27

Avian Flew

A shard of lapis lazuli:
Flashing ruby wings
Caught my eye
As I pulled out of traffic
To contemplate what
I had just seen.
Perhaps the redwinged bluebird
Of which I had long ago dreamed :
Enigmatic, exotic, erotic
All of those and more, worth waiting for.

Grant me that wraith
Avian keeper
And your will be done
By this miserable creeper
Who won't risk your wrath.
Yet when she hovered closer
I realized she wasn't
Blue, but varicoloured
And her hues waxed and waned
Tracking me on her flight path.

Nor were the wings red but
Glowed like burning earth
When they caught
The light and she glistened
In her continuous flight
Just out of my grasp.
And the more I reached
The farther away she swung past
Her parabola undulating
Nearer and farther away

Until I stopped my
Pursuit, and just listened.

I saw an apparition
Through her eyes
The hot burst of pain
A surge of empathy
Not quite a touch
Urging transition
She murmurs, sighs:
"Are you ready?
Come with me."

28

A Near-Perfect World

Thompson both river and setter
Common bonds that
Brought us together.
Tiny ferocious Nicola
The loving glue that held us fast
In a world much fragmented
We feared wouldn't last.

Bisou our first to show us our lot
With cats – Who are not
To be disdained as non-canine.
He won our love through beauty
Swagger and a devotion feline
Finally offering soothing comfort
In murmuring-motor
Lap duty.

Winston was the perfect cat
Wise, kind and so loving that
He thought the world would follow suit.
Too soon he vanished without a sign
Perhaps part of some grand design
To show a near-perfect world
Though fulfilling is not
Without pain and loss, not totally benign.

But the one we have wrought
And continue together to refine.

29

The Journey

The beach was urban
My tirade was disturbin'
When Thompson snagged the attention
Of your empathic soul
Performing a Ciorica intervention
That began in a pub
And quickly expanded - with a kiss
To the wilderness and our own life
Of nonconvention.

From Pasco Road to the downtown eastside
And between we have explored the world
Both New and Old and have seen
How views of life and love can be
As similar as twins as divergent
As faiths and during the journey
We share the revelation that
In continuing discovery
Nothing grows old.

30

Love Song for Dennis Burton

An Eaton's catalogue
Cornucopia of the secrets of
Women in a prePlayboy world
Spread over the prairie skyscape
Shaping the passion of a prepainter
Sketch artist who launched into
The pubescent 50s of Old Canada
Stirring lust, disgust and shaping
Taste, waste and mistrust of
The old ways, order and ordure
Alchemized into aphrodite's essence
As an object of beauty and celebration
Of the pubic, in public, in the mind
Of pubescent boys, pubescent country
Gaining manhood, through womanhood
And feeling good, for once
About it all

31

High Desert, Holy Water

Driving
Through a moonbleached evening
The valley a dystopian landscape
In silver light and shadow
Conjured by a venerable
Tale spinning medicine man.
Testosterone-crazed bighorn sheep
With fire opal eyes
Block my way
Through Spences Bridge
Boiling the blood of
Any big game hunter, not me.

At the Nighthawk Gate
The air pungent with
The scent of sagebrush
Fills my nostrils
Ambrosia to this desert rat
As I pitch the old Eureka Drawtite
Serenaded by coyotes keeping
A respectful distance
And strike a light.

The cliff at Oregon Jack Creek
Across the river
A gigantic drive-in screen
Illuminated by the projector moon
Suddenly erupts, an offering
Another irrigation-triggered avalanche
Thunders into the river.
Too soon,
the moon yields to

A black cloak descending
Into silence.

I feed Thompson S Hunter the setter
Sip a dram of whisky
And watch the fire shrink
To a cache of glowing coals.
A faint rattle reminds me
To resist the urge to hunker down
Under the explosion of summer stars
Perforating an indigo sky.
I crawl into the tent and my dad's old cocoon
Three star down bag that I bought him
And he left me too soon.

Now the dreamless sleep
Shrouds last images
Of steelhead rising to the fly.
So far
The perfect trip
Untouched by tomorrow's reality.

32

The Nighthawk Effect

5:45 a.m.

To the east
The sun rose
Mountain growing gold
To the west
Nicola licked me on the nose

Contessa natters, fishwife true
Driving his lordship from his throne
To soar and swoop low
On a sunning fish
Moving too slow
In the mustard yellow slough.

He returns triumphant provider
And the Contessa – again chatelaine
No longer a shrew
Her beak flashing about
Her voice silenced
By delectable orange ribbons
Of still wriggling trout.

The billowing aroma of
Coffee Sumatra strong
Commands the cabin air
I pour a cup and
Am warmed and soothed
A drink machine-brewed
As I rise from my lair.

Walk, I say
The setters obey
Nicola is lightning
Slicing through new tender shoots,
Over old hardpan
Thompson contentedly sashays
The spike buck watches, stays
For him the world unfolds
According to plan

Above, the osprey surveys
Then strays,
Soaring above the nest
He displays great wings to embrace
A deer, two dogs and a man
Subjects of his realm.

33

Coyote Bacchanal

Under aurora-lit Thompson River sky
A clamour of coyotes shatters the silence
of frozen moonscape. Surging by
Packs rampage through the night
Howling for a mate over hoarfrost-ignited
Sagebrush savannah
They lust to breed, besotted benighted.

Sleepers of the homestead awaken
The shaggy setter sounds the alarm
And dashes for the door
Her sleepy mum follows muttering
Do I have to do this forever more?

My bare feet shuffle over the tiled floor
And I release the hounds.
Josie makes it to the gate in leaps and bounds
Nicola follows suit on the tips of her toes
Not relishing the frost that nips her paws
But loyal to her daughter's neurosis I suppose.

Subzero teeth biting their feet
Freeze their alarm
They retreat to the cabin heat, duty done
Having fended off the harm

We douse the light and resume our repose.

34

The Thrum of the Wild

Living in the downtown eastside
Cristina noted more
Silence
In that city of ceaselessy moving citizens
After the club crowd passed
Than among wilderness denizens.

On the Thompson in the evening
Of the summer solstice
Nighthawks in their dozens
Fill the air with crackling and buzzing
Careering through the sky
Capturing chironimids on the fly
In their millions
Until the sun sinks into the hills
And it becomes too dark
For many more miniscule kills.

Then no sound
Only for a moment
Until the wailing chorale
Of lonesome coyote pups
The cries of bobcats
Marooned on the island
By the spring flood
Pierces the dreams
of sleeping desert rats
A crescending siren
Chilling the blood.

Soon a train as long
As the wagon road

Fills the sound gap
With a distant rumbling clattering rap
Ever higher until it inundates
The world and creates
Its own mesmeric mystery
In that ancient lake bottom
Flowing to the sea.

As the night retreats
A barn owl speaks turning
The gray crepuscular terror red
With its blood curdling shrieks

Finally silence
Then in counterpoint
The Amadeus reveille
The meadowlark is delivering
Assures us that
Not only is another day
Upon us, but that it is
Well worth living.

35

The Huntresses of Nighthawk

They run as a pack
One burnished bronze, two legged
Striding, devouring the moment
Scanning the horizon
Never looking back.

The second, four-legged matriarch
Determined, obsessed, very dark
Forges ahead
And plunges into the lair
To capture the creature
Not part of her mission
Sequestered there.

The third, her daughter
Trots with her
Coursing she flows,
Swallowing scent
Absorbing the world she knows
Her mum and the strider
Beside her.
Whoa! There! An outrider
Now turn and point
To expose.

Gone the terror of claw and fang
Of the catamount that attacked
She bled from a bloody head
But wouldn't go down
And gave chase as her tiny mum snarled
The cat let go and sprang

Into the gnarled cottonwoods
Now replaced by the windborn trace
Of the bird she has tracked.

The genetic imperative in pursuit
She suddenly takes root
Transfixed
And her mum
Betwixt lust for blood and
Inbred command drops
Her hunt for the vole and
Follows suit

To honour the prize and the bronze
Strider
Enflamed beside her
Also complies.

I step forward with pleasure
For they offer the moment to me
To measure.

The copper bell no longer rings
No warning as the silence explodes
In cackles and wings
Life/death, ancient reprise
I swing and squeeze.

The hunt, a symphony, unfolds.

36

Ritual Winter Burn

Dead of winter
Silence
The creak of raven wings overhead
The crunch of setter feet
Shattering ice
On the north field
We torch the scorched
Junipers of a past summer's fire.
The flame explodes melting winter pallor
Searing the death cloak of
An ancient cave dweller's salvation
Heat and light to entice
Spring into an earth
Too long sleeping
Chilled to the core
Now stirring
Preparing
For rebirth.

37

The Fledgling

The river inundates the land
Restores the aquifers
Giving new life to riparian
And savannah. Redemption.
The eagles urge their fledglings
To soar above the river
To land in the territory of fang and claw.
Gigantic babies yet as vulnerable
As the fairylike meadowlarks
Hidden in fields lush
With rye grass and purple sagebrush..
Monstrous infants featherclad
Overshadowing
Anxious mum and dad.

One flies into the jaws of a predator
And perishes before her
Horrified parents.
A scene of terror repeated many times
In the desert
But the second lands softly
And secretly
Outfoxing the trickster of legend
And after an hour's respite
It creaks majestically proud
back to the safety of the aerie

To tell the story that night
To adoring family
Of the maiden flight
And to be fed yet another time
As it preps for strife

beyond the sanctuary of family life
As any living thing must
that rides the rise and fall
Of flood and flame.
Of sun and moon
To end as dust

38

Contessa's Cry

A desperate osprey mum
Repeatedly soars by
Clutching a succulent fish
Past the post where her chick full grown
Sat with its head down -
- to tempt it back to the family.
Today we found on the ground
Her child
Not sick but gone
Victim of eagle or heron

They carry on…trying
One chick still striving within
The cycle of living…and dying.

39

The Maverick

They ranged the mountain above us
Spring escapees, ornery cusses
Horned steers who fought
Lions, bears and would-be
human harvesters.
One was found dead, shot?

In midwinter Cristina got the call
From our neighbour
The truculent survivor
Was in the dry swale
Having spurned the bait: Bales of hay
Laid out in the fall

In favour of foraging for
Remnants of the rich wild grass
Of last summer's providence.

She loaded her Browning 243
Donned her winter gear and
Set out to track down her quarry.
Clearing the woods she spotted him:
There he was a throbbing black engine
Blowing steam
Eyes enflamed with rage
Pawing the ground
Showing no fear at all
On his self-made wilderness death stage.

She steadied her rifle on a downed tree
Sighted in on his shoulder and fired.
The beast crashed, but then

Supernaturally rose again
A shot rang out,
This time he expired.

Startled, she realized the neighbour
Secreted in the woodlot
In her line of fire, had delivered
The kill shot. Much later
She came home with flesh and hide
And pride as hunter-provider
To honour the beast - nurtured in the land-
That she had carved with her own hand.

40

Death of the Fisher Prince

The osprey newly fledged
Clung to the electric pole
His head drooped
Unmoving
Wounded by a marauding eagle
He suffered unwilling unable
To come home.
Mother flew past
Again and again
A trout held firmly in her grasp
Desperate
Agonizing
Trying to tempt her child
To return to the family nest
So close by
His sanctuary past.

Next day
The pole his cenotaph.
He lay strewn
A shattered funerary vase
Shimmering, bronze feathers
Fluttering in the breeze
The prince's remains
Adorning the base.

41

Season's End

Gaunt hills powdered to a funereal pallor
Ride the shores of a current quicksilver thick
Within the Yuletide half moon night
That conceals
Deep in the bathtub anteroom
Of the river
An iron-casqued veteran of the autumn wars
Pondering past terrors of
Tooth and twine and steel
In stoic silence
To wait out the long twilight.
A lone sentinel guarding the tail
Whose lingering passion enflames
His flanks to a Templar's chain mail
Works his kype, burning from the gold and green
Fluttering offering that – at last light – fired
Quinquennial memories of May and stone fly
In this his natal lie.
Now all that remains is the long dream
The greening stones having beckoned
Him to the home stream
Of November
To plant his genes. In spring.
One last task, so few left
To remember.

42

The Enigma

She lies on the shag rug
A cosy 70s relic picked up
At the Mennonite thrift store.
Brit, the unfathomable
Whose blank stare belies
Her surging cyber brain
That at one year of age
While we watched
Two bighorns face off
On the wagon road
At dusk spotted
A herd of ewes
And somehow squeezed out of
The back window of the pickup
And chased them up the mountain.
A tiny speck 1000 feet up
That halted when the killer spikehorns
Turned and formed a phalanx
At the bottom of a scree slope..
We bade her our goodbyes
But she thought the better of it
And turned
Descending to the truck
In less than a minute.

Twice while we cut firewood at the log jam
On the heels of a blood curdling scream
Brit came hurtling out of the underbrush
A coyote in hot pursuit.
Who vanished when I reached for my rifle.
Brit, covered in blood,
mortally wounded we thought

Not so, the blood not hers.
She had been attacked
Turned and ripped out the throat
Of her assailant.
Yet when the wobbling 18 month old
Visiting infant grabbed her by the hair
Of her back and shook her and
His panicking mother shrieked
Brit stood steady as a rock
Eyed her chubby chortling tormentor
And dreamed of that sanctuary
On the shag rug.

43

The Short Happy Life of Nicola De Beauvoir

At the moment
Her plaintive howl began to resound
Through the Tacoma warehouse
Cristina's heart began to pound.
The three month old pup
Was trying to fathom what
Had happened to her
First spirited from home
Into air cargo in Spokane
And finally being abandoned
To the gloom of the
Cavernous Tacoma airdrome.

Cristina vaulted the counter
And rescued the pup from
Her transport kennel hellhole fate
Who immediately fell silent
And closed her eyes in
Those sheltering arms
Activated only when she
Was laid in the grass
And relieved herself
For two minutes straight.
And with a lick of her benefactress's face
Sprang into action
Ready to begin her new life.
A new family to embrace.

Nicola De Beauvoir named
After a tributary of the Thompson
And our UK family
Was greeted graciously by

Thompson S Hunter
Who expected her to leave
As everyone had after three days
But to his dismay he realized: "She stays!"
So he sat in a corner to grieve
Facing the wall feeling strife
What was going to become of
His hitherto, unto then idyllic bachelor life?

Merely a new reality wherein
Nicola defined it with her intense eyes
And a spirit that became heated when
Cristina playfully placed socks on her
And Thompson's feet then
With a withering sigh of exasperation
She removed. First from hers
And then when Thompson did not rebel
Infuriatingly tolerant, from his as well.
A sign that a new regime had entered
That domestic situation.

Our plan had been to extend the line
Of Thompson S Hunter a fine
Gentle companion, relentless bird hunter
And as it turned out, able avenger
For when a Tibetan temple dog
Attacked, he merely tore open its face
And went back to stalking birds even
As the faux bully Sharpe
Ran howling to his human defender.

Our fear was that at seven, Thompson was too old
Or gay as in deference he had shown fondness for
A handsome golden retriever of
no discernible gender preference.
We needn't have worried.

Nicola using her feminine wiles
Worked him relentlessly apace
We returned home one evening
to find them locked
In the traditional doggy style embrace
That in sixty days revealed
Thompson had
At least one active swimmer
And Nicola's water broke in the space
to her apologetic consternation
Under Ehor's desk and within an hour
Josie Bonaparte his reincarnation shot out
and immediately sought out
Nicola's teat and so nourished
By Mother de Beauvoir
To twice her size she flourished.

Nicola's life quest was
to win the heart of any guest
Shamelessly climbing into bed
with any who welcomed her
And swearing undying love
Again and again
Her devotees multiplied and
Her self-esteem, never slight
Swelled to Himalayan height.
She became the queen of her domain.

And soon let everyone know her intent
If she was not completely content
Whining and howling until
The world was re-set to her will.

With Thompson her consort
She became *la reine de la chasse*
Whether pointing chukars for sport

Or hapless turkeys who bore the brunt
Of her ferociousness as she raced past
Her mouth brimming with gobbler quill
Her eyes ablaze with genetic will
Her blood aroused, passion to the last.

She declared herself the fly fisher's ghillie
Retrieving fish brought to the shore
With hardly a tooth mark to amaze
Onlookers both ardent and casual
As she laid them now and then
Before the happy angler's proud gaze.
To be released unharmed to swim again.

Then the flood brought a cursed wreck
Beached on our shore attracting endless drek:
Mice that rattlers and Nicola couldn't resist
One night she abandoned the family pack
She was missed on the way back
From the evening outing
But no amount of calling and shouting
Of searching to find her
Brought a familiar wail
Or sign of our beloved setter grandmother.
Gone without a trace
Sadly we resigned there will never be another.
The heart ache hardly lessens but her legacy
Lives on in essence, in Bella and Brit who
Show glimpses of her highness
In brains, beauty, grit and kindness.

44

The Lion Hunting

She sits invisible
In the logjam den
Where her kittens
Are just starting to
Open their eyes.

She sees the setter pups
Pass by, too risky, and then the coyotes
Stalking them from the high grass.
Again too risky.
She must get food to keep up her strength
But only if that means leaving the kits
For no more than a few minutes.

And then she spots it
A fledgling eagle
On its maiden flight
Gliding across the river from
The aerie on the far side.
It will be exhausted when
it lands near her den.

Now she watches it land
Crying out to its proud parents
Who anxiously watch
As it rests, regains its strength.
A huge creature taller
Than the cougar herself
At the shoulder.

She scans the terrain
No dogs, no coyotes in sight
She waits a few moments
Weighing the pros and cons

And then slinks out of the den

The eaglet having landed
Is preening herself
Regaining strength
When she hears her parents scream.
She looks around and sees the cougar
She must fly, her parents take to the sky

She has not regained her full strength.
But she must get airborne.
The lion is only the length
Of the long log lying on the shore
Away. The eagle child is now
Shrieking in full voice

The lion tenses for the leap
The eagle appears doomed
But then manna from heaven:
A shimmering pink salmon drops near her,
Still wriggling.
The cat is confused, distracted
A new scenario is enacted

As she ponders her options
The giant eaglet wafts aloft
The lioness has hesitated and lost
Then she spots the salmon
And looks skyward where
The eaglet's mama hovers awhile
Having paid a ransom for her child..

The eaglet survives, then
The lion tracks down the bribe
And brings it to her den.
For once no one has to die
for her to be fed to provide
Milk for her budding pride
Other than the salmon, that is.

45

From Sea to Sea By Cell To Cell

The river drops
Clouds of sedges born in the river
Descend upon the junipers
Streamside
I text my son fishing 5000 km away
He answers:
Hi Dad: Rainy?
Has been but finally sunny
Sedges popping here, any luck?

Water temperature too high
In the lower river so I am hiking
To the upper. Bugs bad but salmon
May be there.
Try lemon eucalyptus oil
Will do, heading to upper river now xo
Just lost a large brook trout at the waterfall pool
On a green bomber
Whoa! Good start, record your day.
You won't regret it.

Woohoo! Five more landed
Some nice sized.
All on the bomber.

Holeee! Personal best?
So great to enjoy it with you.
Yes, thanks Dad!
Heading up to the canyon.
Be careful: you're on a roll.

Everything is bonus
Take some river shots
Wow! That is beautiful.
To hell with mowing.
I am going fishing.

Yay! Keep me posted
Next pool fish rising everywhere
Some big ones…
Could only get small to medium to take

Going up to the canyon
Try sedge or mayfly
Unwtd nymph/emerger

Got a few with the mayfly
Now heading into the canyon
Will have to fish dead drift upstream
Hmm, not even a small one in the canyon

They are down where the hatch is on.
Nothing on the dry here at the Beaver Lodge Pool.
Your canyon is gorgeous
Try a bomber..heading downstream
For the evening fish.

Just lost a nice fish at
The Rattlesnake Riviera Pool
On a nymph…and rises happening?
You're just getting into the magic hour.

Lost nice one & one 18 inches on a big caddis nymph
Whoa, nice one dad. Trying to download the picture you sent...
Nicola landed it. She is very gentle, no marks on the fish.
Doesn't look so big due to the angle
but I have marks on my rod for measuring
Got your photos thx
Here is the final one I released
Lots more bites but just little ones...
beautiful fish dad! I miss those rainbows

My bite was just starting but back at the ranch now
and have to work hives later
Oh okay I see
I miss fishing with you for those beautiful brookies
But messaging is the next best thing.
Sharing from sea to sea.
Have a good snooze.
Your big one was at least 16 inches.
Huge for a native wild stream brookie. Congrats
Beautiful river, ever see anyone else?

No

Seasons of the Steelhead
46

Winter Solstice

The rains of November have come and gone
The river swelled and surged and subsided.
We rose in the dark, stoked with coffee and eggs and rashers of bacon
To head up past the gate into the lost world of the watershed.
Silence but for the soft murmur of our boots in the downy snow
And the rhythmic panting of the setters forging ahead…
The last pool before the canyon is suffused with cathedral lighting
The fly flutters, gaudy as its Davie St. namesake
Caressed by the current, engulfed by the gloom
Nothing.
So we push on, higher into the remote reaches
Past rosehips glowing dimly like failing Christmas lights.
To the island pool resplendent in a filigree cloak of hoar frost
Once more the iridescent Hooker vanishes into the riffle
And halts.
A mailed fist bursts through the surface, brandishing a challenge
The ratchet chatters, the rod arcs, the river erupts in the distance
I stumble after over icy stones, conceding line, winding hard
Down the run, past the cribbing, through the chute
It is suddenly before me
An argentite phantom suspended in the stream
The fly glowing in its jaw, a treacherous jewel.
My friend twists out the barb
Back into the river, pause, vanish.
We trudge downstream, elated, complete
Soon reliving the winter wraith again
Over and over before a blazing fire
As a smoky dram soothes us to sleep.

47

The Rites of Spring

A time for the Island, thrumming with the exultation of rebirth
The hillsides are drenched blood-red with salmon berries.
Our spunky Zodiac plunges through the fiord
To a river of absinthe emptying unmolested
Into the sea.
Its maidenhood confirmed by a giant spruce straddlings its banks.
In her estuary our campfire crackles far into the night
Punctuating laughter and song.
Rising languidly at the crack of noon
We wander upriver drifting Woolly Worms though emerald pools
Where strange, tiny steelhead slash viciously
Sparkling diamonds flashing in liquid velvet settings.
Exquisite Lilliputians we send on their way
And rejoice in those denizens of that enchanted waterway.

48

The Perseids Run

We gather in the queasy predawn
Pilgrims about to set off for the Holy Land
Our litany embraces weather, river conditions, news of the run
Grizzlies and logging road washouts

The flight is an exercise in ambivalence
Wonderment at the beauty of the Coastal Range
Of islands sprinkled like asteroids over an indigo infinity.
Then impatience to view the river of so many fantasies
To assuage anxieties on a dozen counts.

We see it now, a braided vein of nephrite
Splitting the mountains to the horizon
We breathe a silent prayer it is fishable.

Somehow we land safely on the stone strewn strip.
An antiquarian Chevy pickup greets us
Its octogenarian driver grinning gaptoothed
Two of us career like spacemen in the back
As we bound over washouts
Branches lashing our faces.

A monstrous silvertipped shadow
Vanishes into the bush on one side.

Canopies of orange and blue welcome us to base camp.
The outgoing crew imparts words of gentle wisdom

Our bodies twitch with a terrible need
To don waders and enter the river

Before it too vanishes,
Before we awaken
Before the steelhead move upstream
We run a gauntlet of devil's club
To find the water low and clear and cool.

I tie on a giant, hirsute immigrant
From the salmon rivers of the east.
The fly lands sparrowlike in the tailout
Of a broad glide.

Mend once, twice, it starts to swing.
Gathering speed, it kicks up a tiny rooster tail
Then disappears.

I swallow hard, the slick explodes
In a shimmering crescent of spring steel.
Our devotions have been answered
I have my miracle.

Night descends in delicious exhaustion.
We laugh, we eat
We lay our backs on the cool sand
Sharing the celebration of the skies
In a shower of cascading stars.

49

Autumn In the Rain Shadow

I glimpsed the river on my migration west
Vast, churning, frothing, a moving sea.
Waters I'll never fish, I thought, shuddering
Dead wrong.
When the autumn monsoon inundates the coast
We head through the mountains to witness the rain shadow
Suck the forest dry, turning lush landscape
Into a dessicated revenant
Spiculated with sagebrush, cactus and juniper.
The cavernous saloon resounds with the clamor of subcultures
Cowhands and Indians, a raucous gang of railroaders
And wanderers of the 13th tribe
Who mark the season by the river they are on
Wintle, Winters, Lemire, Kambeitz and Maisonpierre
Gentle, jovial, taciturn, sage and arrogant by turn
Esteemed devotees of the art of steelheading.
Last night's puddles splinter under our cleats as we approach
Far out in the glide colossal forms are porpoising in the half light
The hissing of lines caresses a silence
Shattered by an express train thundering upstream
And Grisewood's ululating above the din
His rod high he is fast to an underwater locomotive
Steaming downstream.
His prayer answered, his *cauchemar* darkens the horizon
Impossibly far below him
I wind in, this river is unforgiving
And the primal battle has just begun.

50

The Dean

Ted Hughes
Through the Campfire Smoke

Flashes of light
A fusillade from the ambush of paparazzi
Punctuate the gloom of a London May morning.
We move through the onlookers
To the great doors of Westminster Abbey
Soaring gothic columns resounding
With the sonorous waves of a Bach fugue
A hand on my sleeve, "Dad, I don't feel too well.
I glance at Alexei, my twelve year old son.
His normally cherubic face is ashen.
His sister, Jennifer, recognizes the symptoms
Gently bids him place his head
Between his knees.
His first time in a great medieval church
Redolent with the sound of organ and voice,
He is nearly overcome.
"It's like heaven," he whispers.

We rise as the royal family enters,
The Queen Mother as lovely and fragile
As an autumn leaf
On the arm of her grandson, the Prince of Wales.

There are nineteen hundred of us and much music
The Adagio from Beethoven's Sonata No. 17
Played by Alfred Brendel.
At the close, the haunting melody of Spem in Alium
Sung by the Tallis Singers.

"
.

For Ted Hughes, British Columbia was
The road not taken
Around our campfire on the Dean,
A barrage of northern lights rippling and crackling overhead
He said how coming to BC had rekindled a part of him
Long dormant
Since his brother had moved away
And that in spirit and gesture,
I reminded him of his brother.

In the abbey, speakers read from Ted's works.
The poems, nightmarish memories
Of the first world war
Left unspoken, haunting Ted's father,
Anniversary:
The death of his mother 'in her feathers of flame"
And That Morning:
Watching salmon in a stream
Conjuring boyhood memories
Endless flights of bombers
filling the night sky.
His words fill the abbey
Igniting even more..

Seamus Heaney stands before us in the abbey intoning:
Ted was a great man and a great poet
through his wholeness, simplicity and truth
to his world
A world epic and stern,
Beholding behind the business of the usual,
a sacred drama:
Everything that wanted to live, whether cell or salmon,
was hurling itself over the top
in wave after gallant wave...
He recognized the body was born for ecstasy …and extinction.

Heaney's words reflect a poem he never read:
The Bear, written by Ted,
a logbook entry on the Dean
Describing a storm:

Everything was worsening.
But we sat there
And enjoyed it. And the Steelhead down there
They were enjoying it too, this was what they were made of,
And made by, and made for, this was their moment.
The thousand-mile humping of mountains
That looked immovable, was in a frenzy,
Metabolism of stars, melt of snows -
Was shivering to its ecstasy in the Steelhead.
This actually was the love-act that had brought them
Out of everywhere, squirming and leaping,
And that had brought us too - besotted voyeurs -
Trying to hook ourselves into it.
And all the giddy orgasm of the river
Quaking under our feet

Heaney goes on to place Ted
In the pantheon of great poets
From Caedmon to Shakespeare and Hopkins.
When he leaves the podium
There is silence.
Then a powerful Yorkshire voice fills the abbey:
"Fear no more the heat of the sun."
It is Ted reading from Shakespeare's Song of Cymbeline:
"Golden lads and girls all must,
As chimney sweepers,
Come to dust."

I hear once again his voice as he lay on his back
By the campfire at Basque on the Thompson River
Pointing out the Perseids meteor showers

To a very young Alexei,
Regaling us all with ghost stories,
His spirit spilling over with joy
Rediscovering the universe
Through the eyes of a child.
On my grand-daughter's first birthday he penned a verse
that we stuck on a rocket and fired off over Howe Sound.
to assure good fortune, no copy was kept.
Some secrets of the universe one does not trifle with..

Later, we discussed what we would do differently
If we had our lives to begin again.
I presumed Ted would not change his career as a poet.
Not so, he said softly: "I might want to come back as a Sufi."
A Sufi? One who meditates on the secrets of the universe,
pursuing inner truth and peace
imparting insights to the people in stories?
A light year away from the public glare
of being Poet Laureate.

"Here," said Jerry Rogers, decades ago,
my friend and prose editor at Western U's Folio mag
"Something for a northern Ontario boy."
A collection of Robert Service poems?
Not exactly. It is *Lupercal* by Ted Hughes
And then I read Hawk Roosting:

I sit in the top of the wood, my eyes closed.
Inaction, no falsifying dream
Between my hooked head and hooked feet:
Or in sleep rehearse perfect kills and eat...

The sun is behind me.
Nothing has changed since I began.
My eye has permitted no change,
I am going to keep things like this.

I am transfixed, then transported.
He is writing about my childhood
Life and death in fang and claw.
There is an immediacy in reading his poetry
That rivals the experience of actual wilderness,
Of wild animals going about making a living,
And that, but for the grace of God,
You might be part of
That unfiltered experience
In Yukon
As grizzlies wander about
In Vancouver's downtown eastside
Where drug dazed denizens wander about
All hunting and gathering

Fifteen years later, I send off a batch of my writing
To New Yorker Nick Lyons,
He writes back asks if I know Ted Hughes,
an Englishman who married Sylvia Plath?
He is, a better poet.
And cites Hughes' October Salmon:

He's lying in poor water, a yard or so depth of poor safety …
Death has already dressed him
In her clownish regimental, her badges and decorations,
Mapping the completion of his service,
His face a ghoul-mask, a dinosaur of senility, and his whole body
A fungoid anemone of canker

I avoid meeting literary heroes
Lest their personalities be less stellar
Than their work,
Sponsoring a reading by young Leonard Cohen
Yet opting not to meet him face to face. A pity.
Now I decide to risk it
Send Hughes a cycle of poems:
The Seasons of the Steelhead

I. Winter Solstice
The rains of November have come and gone
The river swelled and surged and subsided.
We rose in the dark, stoked with coffee and eggs and rashers of bacon
To head up past the gate into the lost world of the watershed.
Silence but for the soft murmur of our boots in the downy snow
And the rhythmic panting of the setters forging ahead...

Months pass
Then I get a letter from Alaska.
It is from Ted Hughes,
Sitting in a cabin in the Alaska bush
Visiting his son,
He writes in ball point on
Alaska Cooperative blue stationery:

Dear Ehor Boyanowsky,
Your letter to me was so full of things that I've been saving my answer till
I had time (and peace of mind) to do it justice. Most of my life now (since
I was dubbed Laureate) is spent writing letters I do not want to write at
all. But now here I am in Alaska far from your letter and poems. You can
imagine, nothing could be more to my taste than what you write about.
So from what you showed me, I'm probably one of your keenest fans...

I'm writing now in the hope of getting some sort of letter to you before I
get to Victoria on the 16th. I'm giving a reading there on the night of the
18th, then again in Vancouver on the 19th. If it's the sort of thing you go to,
I'd love to say hello.

I have been to many poetry readings.
Held in cobweb ridden bookstores or classrooms
With the ambience and roominess of broom closets.
They are never standing room only.
In The University of British Columbia Music Recital Hall,
Hundreds of people are already seated.
Dozens, many with granny glasses and crocheted toques

adorning their ratty coiffures, are milling about in a quandary outside.
They did not expect such a grand venue to be completely sold out
They are left to wait in the foyer for the reception.
This is a giant space made for orchestras and great choirs.
I don't even know the man,
I worry about how one voice merely reading poetry
will command the attention of the multitude
in this cavernous room.

A veritable giant,
Moving with geological force,
A shard of the cliffs of Dover broken off,
Dressed in the tweedy brown
Of the nondescript Englishman,
Mounts the podium.
He starts to speak in a deep, rumbling gentle voice
Silence falls upon the room.
He describes each poem's provenance
Verse that on the page was obscure
Now transparent as crystal.
Hughes describes how one night,
Struggling with a literary critique,
He has a dream of a fox with a severed, bloody head
Standing at the foot of his bed.
It tells him, "You're killing me, you're killing me."
His psyche is warning him that should he continue
To study English literature, his creative spirit,
What Garcia Lorca called *duende*,
Will soon be exhausted,
Used up in sterile activity.
He transferred into anthropology.
For him writing poems is like hunting animals,
And then he reads The Thought Fox:

I imagine this midnight moment's forest:
Something else is alive
Beside the clock's loneliness
And this blank page where my fingers move...

Till with a sudden sharp hot stink of fox
It enters the dark hole of the head.
The window is starless still; the clock ticks,
The page is printed.

The hall is silent,
So quiet that the soft sucking sounds of a breastfeeding Alexei
Can be heard distinctly,
I am amazed.
And I understand now how women, and men too,
Fall in love with Hughes, shy as he is,
For once he gives of himself,
He holds nothing back.

The river is low and cool and clear
We row over to the shaded left bank of the Victoria Run.
The ululant victory cries of our campmates,
Hooking steelhead resound in our ears
Ted and I trundle downstream over the cobbles
I don't mention to Ted,
Most Europeans, almost paranoid
About the danger posed by bears,
That only last week, on the spot we have chosen to fish,
A septuagenarian long time Dean River aficionado
Had been charged by a mother grizzly
As he sprinted downstream fighting, the "mother of all steelhead."
Refusing to break off the fish, he argued that he had lived long enough
But never before had had a chance to land such a behemoth
. He kept running downstream until the grizzly finally gave up the chase,
rearing up on her hind legs and roaring as she shook her shaggy head

We fish with dry flies.
They require very aggressive fish,
Only those tempted to rise to the surface will respond to the fly.
"Like making love with the lights on" I explain.
Several casts bring no surges from the depths,

We hear more maddening victory cries from our companions
It is one thing not to be catching fish.
It is another much more painful experience
While one's companions are hooking fish after fish
"Okay, Ted, enough is enough.
Put on a sinking tip line and a Squamish Poacher
I shall put on a Davie St. Hooker."
Ted does as he is told, his powerful meathook hands
Engulfing the gaudy bauble
He fastens to his leader.
"Sometimes they just have their noses buried in the gravel,
Especially if they have been there awhile"
"And you have to bring the fly to them."
"Turning off the lights, are we Ehor?"
"I am afraid so Ted,.
"Better to have sex in the dark than not at all."

Ted lifts his powerful fifteen foot river jousting rod
Fires the fly into the current
I become the ghillie
On the third cast, Ted's rod tip dips
He is into a lovely fish, not large but very silvery and aerial,
Hurtling itself out of the river six or seven times
Before he brings it to shore.
In Europe, salmon fishing is about killing fish
I watch anxiously as he unhooks the steelhead
Panting quite rapidly, crouches on his knees,
Admiring it and repeating in a kind of thanksgiving mantra:
"Thank you Ehor, thank you, for bringing me to my first steelhead,
She is surpassingly beautiful.

"Well done Ted, but let's row back across
To the camp". I had spotted a massive shadow
In the forest behind us watching
And the putrid musky odor of a grizzly
Permeated the air.

It would not do to lose the Laureate
On his first day on the Dean.

My friend orders Ted to start the fire
While he prepares the nose thumbing
Impractical feast of fresh crab and prawns and scallops
And basmati rice and a delicious curry
An affront to the traditional menu
Of more seasoned veterans
Who pack only canned meats and vegetables.

Aperitifs of gin and tonics,
Fine BC and Chilean wines
To wash down the feast
And drams of single malt
Make the crackling flames
Growing ever larger
A portal into our psyches.

We speak of everything but fishing
Girding my loins I ask Ted
What the issue was with his former wife.
"She has become a victim of male oppression
In the minds of some women
Whereas the reality is she was willing to
Unhinge the world to achieve what she wanted"
And what was that?
"Everything: love, fame, children, writing that
Had enduring meaning, beginning with her
Hatred of her father for dying, and her mother for
Dominating, choking her life.
All driven by the fear that she would be abandoned
Did not deserve the gift of anyone's love.

Was your relationship violent?
"It began with her biting me, drawing blood

I became completely smitten
And when we came together it was the perfect
Symbiosis. I wrote and she typed and sent it out.
She struggled to find topics but when she did
Sometimes with my help
She produced magic and we fed on each other's
Energy. It was like living in a conflagration."
So exquisite, painful, satisfying,
I shall never recapture it."

So you never struck her?
"Never in anger. Only when she
Became hysterical with jealousy
Of a coed she saw me with walking across campus,
Of a matronly BBC producer with whom
I lunched a bit too long discussing a project.
She would pummel me, scratch me, tear up my manuscripts
She was very strong and I could not hold her
So I slapped her. And she would awake
As from a fugue state. And apologize.
Until the next time.

"Finally, she invited home a very beautiful woman
Who made me a target, a project and by then
I was easy pickings. 'Like taking candy from a baby'
She apparently told friends. I still needed the *duende*
Only Sylvia gave me
But it was too late. I didn't answer the phone the night
She killed herself."

I knew the story, the others didn't
There was a long dense silence
As the flames licked at the dry spruce.
Sparks resounded like gunshots in the silent dark.
"What happened to her?" asked my friend.
"She was torn between me and her husband,"

Her obsession was to outdo Sylvia. She killed herself
In the same way."

A silent gasp passed around the fire.

"And the child she said was mine."
Sometimes one regrets the questions one asks
In the intimacy of the campfire.
No one moved, no one took a sip, no one said a word.

"My life has been an open wound since.
I bury myself in raising my children,
In my scribbling and in fishing.
They are my analgesics, my opium
As I swing between intense purging,
like my story of Gaudete,
A tortured alter ego I invented to expiate the guilt.
It didn't really work. So I keep searching for muses wherever
I can find them. Each one keeps me going…until they no longer do."

And tomorrow the steelhead will be surging upstream
To make it all worthwhile, I add.
A clap of thunder, then the downpour begins.

51

Deliverance Redux: On the Babine

We enter the rift valley of the river
A child of the Pleistocene when glaciers grew
Then receded and tectonic plates clashed
Tipping on end to leave
Sheer walls of granite
Creating the cathedral of the Babine.

Myriad sockeye
Shimmering living rubies
Clamouring at the counting fence
Black Friday shoppers in odyssey
Seeking the least expense, the best deal
To ensure the enduring survival
Revival of their own progeny.

Shaggy gangs of grizzlies gather
On the shelves of steep cliffs
Cubs tucked in trees
Boars, sows claiming their stations
Roaring and scaring off wannabes, lesser relations.
They prepare to snare the salmon
On catcher jaws, razor claws, to devour their brains
Protein to dream in hibernation
During the long boreal winter
Of unending future salmon migration.

We drift past in respectful silence
A phantasmagoria of
Yellow rafts, blue tunics and green slickers
That Ursus Horribilis barely notes askance
Beady eyes focused on the back eddy
At his feet. We are mere river flotsam
To him. Not worthy of a glance.

Fine with us
As our cameras click and our
Plans turn to the campsite downstream
Too soon we feel the shock of alarm
As the raft which had
Previously slid off
Midstream boulders without harm
Is sucked against one newly exposed
by the thin riverine flow the drought has imposed.
It thrums like a wounded beast
Impaled on a medieval fortress siege machine.

The second raft pulls to shore and a line is cast
To the stricken craft that the guide catches and attaches.
The four of us heave to, pulling to save the boat, the trip
Our newfound companions. The raft holds fast
Then slowly moves sideways and slips past the rock.
We are free to continue our journey into the bowels
Of the canyon.

That chilly evening, after a guide-prepped meal of delish fajitas
A glass of wine and a dram of scotch to heat us
We chuckle around the fire, reliving the sirenlike treachery
That could have dispersed us insidiously
But in the end bonded two groups
Better than hugs: shared adversity.

I rise at dawn from a dreamless sleep
Prints in the sand reveal
A brobdingnagian patrol
Graciously chose not to impose.
Donning my waders and boots and my
Lance-like double hander I wonder aloud:
Where to fish?
To the riffle around the bend.
Out of sight of the sleeping crowd.
Perfect fly water –Stretching the leader on it I tie
A Thompson River Rat, my version of the Miramichi Bomber dry fly.

A relic from my eastern past, hoary, hirsute
It lands sparrowlike on the seam
And on the tenth cast I feel the line grow tight
I have my dream: a great Babine steelhead
Surges downstream with me in pursuit.
Minutes later it pulses in the shallows for one photo
Regaining strength, it wrests its tail from my grasp
And shatters into deep amber river light.
An NBA chest pound echoes through the canyon.
Bravado I had disdained, now feels just right. Apropos.
Another two. Time to go.

I return to the camp where my friend drying dishes
Drops the towel upon hearing of my successes
And stumbles downstream. He returns smiling in an hour
Having hooked an eighteen pounder. And another.
A new chapter in steelhead pilgrim history
We join the others, our faces beam
Hearts swelling, serene, having solved this river mystery.

At Grizzly Drop in helmets and neoprene gear
The rafters ride the cataract,
Screaming soundlessly, completely soaked
Moments later, out of the froth they reappear
River-doused, adrenaline stoked.

And then drift, silently through Kisgegas Canyon
At the suspension bridge, we climb the sheer wall
Out of the shadowy grotto into a meadow of early fall
Bucolic serenity, sunshine, trees of rattling gold doubloons
Melancholy, ravished by small pox a century ago
Heartbreaking beauty of graves, church, cabins, crumbling ruins.

We paddle in silence pondering the village of wraiths
At the bottom of the canyon an impasse,
Too narrow this last Kesgegas crevasse, for the bulging pontoons

We unload the rafts, deflate them to slimmer waists
Barely squeeze through the dessicated flow now snail paced.

Under the bridge, the cringeworthy roar
of logging trucks we can only deplore
Assails our senses, deflates our spirits,
Incites fear and begs the question in future to guide us
Will the wild Babine survive the ministrations of man
By the minions of Midas?

On the Skeena
We rise under bleeding skies before dawn
To a chorus of wolves
Urging, pleading that the world must cling desperately anon
To rivers like the Babine
No man, no corporation, no government,
Can replace by reconstruction
The fish, the bears, the ancient trees, the insects
Once they are gone.
Those are the economics, the true cost of destruction.
In silence, we paddle on.

*

52

River Nocturne

No moon tonight
I enter the oaken canopy concert hall
No fragments of light from the farmstead
The river kettle drums rise and fall
A counterpoint to the fluting of the Nightingales
And the bassooning of the owl wafting overhead
My hand has vanished, no skin, no veins no nails.

In Patagonia, roaring wind and icy horizontal rain
Wagnerian harpies shrieking sturm and drang
Mask the threat, banish the fright
Embolden seatrout to attack the fly in broad daylight.

Not here, near Wordsworth's wishing gate.
Only the shroud of blackest night
The soothing unbroken harmony of the nocturne
Impels the cautious sewin to bite.

Downstream the clash of cymbals sounds
The river, strings of current plucked, resounds
Driven to crescendo by the surging silver pod
I unfurl the line and raise the rod
The concert is mine to conduct.

53

For Mary and Sam

Sixty summers ago
Veins of Viking and Celt
Conflowed,
And the River McGinn
Enriched the earth
Winding through the hills of Kilmacolm.

The eddies flowered offspring strong and rooted
Lifted heads of auburn and gold
Marrying stream and bank.
Winds of passing seasons
Sowed their seeds over the spring currents.

The river's mouth
Gave them to the Atlantic.
They drifted to a world new and old,
Threading unknown rivers
Sinking roots in unfamiliar eddies
Where seeds gathered from many lands
Mingled their strengths, and flowered afresh
Lifting again heads of gold and auburn.

Now September winds bend them
Toward the home shore
Remembering the parents' dream
Which still gleams among the home hills.

EOB (edited by Ted Hughes)

54

Mustang

Shaggy, unkempt
Burdocks encrust his
Mane and tail
And his eyes bulge
With threat and quail
Out of an oversized head
Upon my approach.
Feigning ferociousness
In reality skittish with fear.
He wants the apple but
Is loath to let me come near.

Native to the New World
Almost wiped out
By the invading tribes
With their hi-tech weapons,
Stout spears with points
tempered by fire
They crossed the bridge
at Bering Strait and spread southward
Now able to kill at will the fleeing herd.

His ancestors
A few survivors,
Made their escape
To the Old World
Just before they were
Completely laid waste.
Now they are back and
Acute instinct long imbedded
Warns him off two legged

Creatures who once crept
With only a sharpened burnt
Stick to do their bloody work.

Tamed, not killed, nourished
By the wiser Mongols
They flourished, allowed the Khans
To subdue the known world including
Europe where the Spanish crowns
Much later intruding into a world unmapped
Rode the horse to terrify,
To slaughter whole cities entrapped by
Spanish bloodsoaked obsession
With El Dorado legend,
A city of gold
to this day, uncapped.

Now he was back home, a stallion
Wild, free, unbroken by his old enemy
A creature those tribes still strive to recruit:
The mustang pondered: Should he take the fruit ?.

55

The Converts

1. For John Reeves

Gentle Warrior

The young man watched
The US jet swoop low
Over the trees and release
Two incendiary bombs.
Within a human heartbeat
A wall of napalm flame engulfed
The woods, the fields, anything living.
The man, an officer, put down
His AR-15, sat enrapt, grieving
As banshees on fire,
Screaming in horrific pain
Burning before his eyes
To searing black fragments of flesh
Ran toward him
Backlit by the vast funeral pyre.

His past - Proud Texan, a son of the land
Football and track, the Reeves clan, a patriotic band
Honed to do the right thing,
Not to cower before fate
Regardless of the dictate of the state -
Had brought him to this awakening
To surrender to those in command
And profess he could no longer
Kill human beings just because
They were there and his country
Did declare war on their doctrines.

Facing a sentence in prison by law
He took his case to the highest court in the land

And to his and his country's surprise.
They listened to his story and
Agreed he needn't compromise.
The first ever confirmed
Battlefield conscientious objection.
He spent the rest of his life in enlightened
Academic reflection, applying his mind
To science, no blood to spill, not to kill
But to reduce human suffering. And
To promote the good of humankind.

2. For Bill Brough

The Long Journey to Hell and Back

The choice was his
To leave school and work
Where Vulcan ruled
In the bowels of the earth
Or to come to the aid
Of his democratic land
Beset by the axis of evil
Spawned by the rebirth
Of Germany and Japan.
But how? He could not kill
His fellow man.

How then to serve the Allies in their sacred enterprise ?
To hunt down in its lair and exterminate there
The 'rough beast slouching toward Bethlehem.'

He joined the war in the guise
Of the Friends Ambulance corps
A Quaker combat team tooled
Not to kill but to save lives
In the depths of the steaming jungle
Where the Nipponese Satan ruled:
Burma, Hell on Earth, where

The worst forms of cruelty
Creative atrocity: torture
Agony were served by the minions
of Lucifer as standard fare.

The young Englishman braved
The machine gun burst
To reach a Kachin tribesman
Wounded in an attack.
To get him to a field hospital
He'd slung him on his back
Hoping for the best, fearing the worst.

A merciless sniper opened fire
Reduced his living burden
To a lifeless cadaver
And that would-be rescuer to a beast of war.
Bill Brough joined the US special corps
Transformed by outrage into an assassin
Behind enemy lines in the Burmese Abaddon
He killed Japanese with dispassion.

Many men lost their ability
To feel empathy with their enemy
But Brough retained enough humanity
Not to slaughter the Japanese officer
His squad sighted on the last day
Of World War II hostility.
Saving one life.

Awarded the US Presidential Medal for his ferocity
He went on to become a doctor of psychiatry
Dedicated to relieving the psychic anguish
Of his patients, working to restore sanity,
One person at a time
Among a wounded humanity.

56

At Nighthawk

As darkness falls
The mountain across the valley ignites:
A semblance of medieval army encampment
Hundreds of campfires in the night
Breathtaking, exquisite and deadly
Sagebrush explodes and takes flight
Siege machines launched by the onrushing inferno
The juggernaut of flame surges steadily on
And the brave firefighting forces
Sent to subdue this fire storm
Retreat until the dawn
Having evacuated everyone
Or so they think. All gone none lost
Unaware that in anonymous isolation
We are here mere pilgrims to Armageddon
sipping gin and tonics
And pondering without consternation
How to escape the holocaust.